HARRY STYLES

HARRY STYLES

Chart-Topping Musician and Style Icon

HEATHER E. SCHWARTZ

LERNER PUBLICATIONS ◆ MINNEAPOLIS

To my superstar husband, Philip Schwartz

Lerner Publications Company
An imprint of Lerner Publishing Group, Inc.
241 First Avenue North
Minneapolis, MN 55401 USA

For reading levels and more information, look up this title at www.lernerbooks.com.

Main body text set in Rotis Serif Std 55 Regular. Typeface provided by Adobe Systems.

Editor: Brianna Kaiser **Designer:** Connie Kuhnz

Library of Congress Cataloging-in-Publication Data

Names: Schwartz, Heather E., author.
Title: Harry Styles : chart-topping musician and style icon / Heather E. Schwartz.
Description: Minneapolis : Lerner Publications, 2024. | Series: Gateway Biographies | Includes bibliographical references and index. | Audience: Ages 9-14 | Audience: Grades 4-6 | Summary: "Harry Styles is more than an English singer and songwriter. Follow his career from performing with One Direction to becoming a solo artist. Then discover his acting career and how he became a fashion icon"—Provided by publisher.
Identifiers: LCCN 2022049926 (print) | LCCN 2022049927 (ebook) | ISBN 9781728491776 (library binding) | ISBN 9798765602973 (paperback) | ISBN 9781728497662 (ebook)
Subjects: LCSH: Styles, Harry, 1994- —Juvenile literature. | Singers—England—Biography—Juvenile literature. | LCGFT: Biographies.
Classification: LCC ML3930.S89 S23 2023 (print) | LCC ML3930.S89 (ebook) | DDC 782.42166092 [B]—dc23/20221018

LC record available at https://lccn.loc.gov/2022049926
LC ebook record available at https://lccn.loc.gov/2022049927

Manufactured in the United States of America
1-53116-51126-2/28/2023

Table of Contents

Harry Styles gives a speech at the 2021 Grammy Awards after winning the award for Best Pop Solo Performance.

Dressed in a plaid jacket with a purple feather boa around his neck and a matching plaid mask over his mouth, Harry Styles was as stylish as ever at the 2021 Grammy Awards. Among the audience filled with high-profile celebrities, Harry clapped for award winners. But the crowd was small and seated at round tables that gave them space for social distancing. It was the safest way to hold an event during the COVID-19 global pandemic.

Then it was time for the Best Pop Solo Performance award. Harry Styles had been nominated for his song "Watermelon Sugar." It had become a popular summer song during a difficult time for the world. Videos of Styles and the other talented award nominees—Justin Bieber, Doja Cat, Billie Eilish, Dua Lipa, and Taylor Swift—played on-screen in front of the audience. A clip from Styles's "Watermelon Sugar" music video showed him having fun on a beach, singing, laughing, and, of course, eating watermelon. If he won, it would be his first Grammy.

The audience waited eagerly as Rachelle Erratchu, manager of the iconic Troubadour nightclub in West Hollywood, opened the envelope with the name of the winner inside. When she announced Styles as the winner, Styles removed his mask, revealing a smile that lit up his face as he made his way to the stage. Everyone could see his excitement.

Styles with his Grammy award on March 14, 2021

"I feel very grateful to be here, thank you," he said, gesturing to the audience and praising all of the songs that were nominated. "I feel very honored to be among all of you."

His humble delivery matched the mood of the room, which was quiet in light of the pandemic. The win marked his success as a solo artist. Styles had come a long way from his early days singing harmonies in a band to taking center stage on his own.

Life Before Fame

Harry Edward Styles was born on February 1, 1994. He grew up in Holmes Chapel, a village in Cheshire, England. By the time he was seven, his parents, Desmond Styles and Anne Twist, had divorced, but the family stayed close. Harry's parents gave him an early education in different types of music. With his dad, he listened to bands like the Rolling Stones, Fleetwood Mac, Queen, and Pink Floyd. His mom introduced him to the sounds of Shania Twain, Savage Garden, and Norah Jones.

Harry also learned the joys of dressing up from his mom, who loved to see him and his big sister, Gemma, in costumes. One time his mom made a giant papier-mâché mug and painted an atlas on the side, dressing Harry as the World Cup. Another time, he was a dalmatian in a hand-me-down costume, while Gemma was dressed as Cruella de Vil. "As a kid I definitely liked fancy dress," he said.

Styles grew up in Holmes Chapel, a village in England.

The first time he dressed in costume was for a school play. He was a church mouse. He was shocked and thrilled to pull on a pair of tights for the role. In addition to acting, he loved singing. He practiced with a karaoke machine his grandfather had given him. He was always up for entertaining people and making them happy. But there was one area of his life where Harry didn't feel confident: schoolwork. While he was popular and had decent grades, Gemma's grades were better. He was jealous. Harry thought this meant she was smarter than he was.

As Harry and Gemma got older, their mom wanted them to be independent. They came home after school to an empty house while his mom was working. Harry learned to get along with his sister, make pasta for dinner, and cheer up his mom when she got home from work after having a bad day.

One of Harry's first jobs as a teenager was delivering newspapers. He also worked at a bakery. Even though it meant getting up early, he enjoyed working because he liked having money to spend on new, trendy clothes. He went through an early emo phase, wearing skinny jeans and studded belts in a style inspired by emo music. By high school his look was going in a new direction.

He had a new way to express himself too, as the lead singer in a pop punk band. Playing mostly covers—along with a few originals—Harry and his friends performed at weddings and school concerts. They had fun, but by sixteen years old Harry wasn't planning on a career as a singer. He had ideas for a career

Harry Styles at three years old

as a physiotherapist, someone who treats injuries and conditions that affect movement, or maybe a lawyer. He also thought he might study sociology or business.

Then Harry and his friends entered a Battle of the Bands contest—and won! Suddenly, Harry had a different view of what his future could become. "Winning the battle of the bands and playing to that many people really showed me that's what I wanted to do," he said. "I got such a thrill when I was in front of people singing. It made me want to do it more and more."

Styles with his older sister, Gemma Styles, at an event in 2016

It was Harry's mom who saw a path he could follow to get there. She convinced Harry to audition for the United Kingdom's music competition show *The X Factor* in 2010. The show had three judges: record executive and entrepreneur Simon Cowell, singer and songwriter Nicole Scherzinger, and music manager Louis Walsh. Harry appeared confident as he introduced himself to the judges and answered their questions.

"Singing's what I want to do," he said to an interviewer before getting on the stage. "If people that can make that happen for me don't think I should be doing that, then it's a major setback in my plans."

Harry gave his all to his performance of Train's "Hey, Soul Sister." But something seemed off. His voice was pitchy. His singing didn't seem to match the backing track. Luckily, Cowell offered him another chance, asking him to try again without it. This time, Harry sang an a cappella–without instruments–version of Stevie Wonder's "Isn't She Lovely."

The crowd went wild. Walsh gave him a no, but it didn't matter. Scherzinger and Cowell said yes. Harry was going to have the chance to get professional coaching and compete on television for the ultimate prize of a recording contract. If he won, he'd have connections, fans, and a ready-made career as a singer.

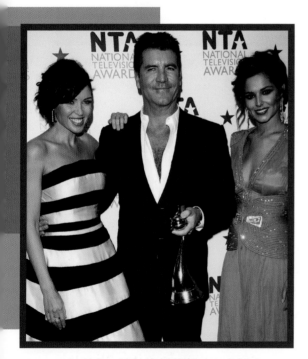

Simon Cowell (*center*) was a judge on *The X Factor* when Harry competed on the show. Here Cowell attends an event with singers Dannii Minogue (*left*) and Cheryl (*right*) in 2010.

Left to right: Liam Payne, Louis Tomlinson, Zayn Malik, Harry Styles, and Niall Horan attend rehearsals for *The X Factor* in 2010.

How The X Factor *Figured In*

Harry had always enjoyed singing for his family and liked performing on stages. But after making it through the first round on *The X Factor*, he became shy. He practiced at home, and he didn't want his sister or their mom to hear him. He hid in the bathroom so no one could see him while he sang. In the past, he'd put on an act, imitating other singers, including Elvis. But as a new solo artist, he was embracing his own style and letting his real voice shine. His performance was becoming a lot more personal.

Harry was prepared and passionate about this next step, but as it turned out, that wasn't enough. At the end of the second stage of the competition, he stood in a line with the other contestants and waited to hear which of them would go on. When the last name was called, it wasn't Harry's. He'd been eliminated. He was devastated.

But this wasn't the end of the road for him on *The X Factor.* Four other talented teenage boys had auditioned as solo artists too, and also didn't get through the second stage. Behind the scenes, Scherzinger, Cowell, and Walsh were brainstorming. What if Harry and these other boys all sang together?

"They're just too talented to get rid of," Scherzinger said. "And they've got just the right look and the right charisma on stage."

Harry was matched up with Zayn Malik, Louis Tomlinson, Niall Horan, and Liam Payne to continue competing on *The X Factor.* Suddenly, instead of going solo, Harry was getting to know his bandmates and learning new songs with them. He came up with a name for their group: One Direction. Six weeks later, they sang Natalie Imbruglia's "Torn" to Cowell. Then they waited anxiously to find out if they would get to continue on the show.

"Your hunger for it grows and grows as you get through each stage of the competition," Harry said. "It's just the biggest stage to be told yes or no. And it's—it's one word that can change your life forever, because it won't be the same if you get a yes. And if you get a no, then it's straight back to doing stuff that kind of drives you to come here in the first place."

On December 9, 2010, Cowell and One Direction attend a press conference for *The X Factor*.

When Cowell told them they'd made it through, the boys cheered. Harry raced to hug Cowell. Harry's life was on track to change forever—in exactly the way he wanted. Everything was falling into place, but the competition on *The X Factor* was fierce.

In December 2010, the show came down to three finalists: Matt Cardle, Rebecca Ferguson, and One Direction. The last two acts would compete head-to-head, and there could be only one winner. The crowd went wild as Matt's name was announced, and Harry bowed his head. There was one spot left.

When Rebecca's name was called, she looked shocked. Cowell turned around in disappointment. Harry started clapping. But it was a devastating moment for every member of One Direction. Clips of their previous performances and victories throughout the competition played for the audience. It was hard to believe their journey on the show was over.

But it was not the end of Harry's musical journey. After working together for months on the show, One Direction had their sound down and a solid base of fans. Harry and his bandmates wanted to continue as a group. They signed on to Cowell's record label Syco Music.

Harry the Heartthrob

During their time on *The X Factor*, the members of One Direction lived together in a rented London, England, mansion. They

recorded video diaries, giving fans a chance to get to know them better. Fans learned that Harry's favorite song was John Mayer's rendition of "Free Fallin'" by Tom Petty and that he could play the kazoo. The band also revealed that Harry was the flirt of the group.

Styles in 2012

One Direction performs on their Up all Night tour in 2012.

Launching with One Direction

One Direction's first album, *Up All Night*, was released in Ireland and the UK in 2011 and globally in 2012. It quickly shot to No. 1 on the *Billboard* 200 albums chart. Styles's life as a singer was launched. Instead of working at a bakery and going to school, he was headlining the Up All Night tour, meeting and talking with celebrities, and building his career.

The band was so successful that Styles bought a home of his own at eighteen years old. He paid about $4.8 million for a place in London.

A Learning Experience

In 2012 singers Taylor Swift and Selena Gomez watched One Direction perform from backstage at the Kids' Choice Awards. Rumors began circulating that Styles and Swift were romantically involved. Soon they were dating, and the media widely covered their relationship. Their romance didn't last long, and when asked about it later, Styles called it a learning experience. He kept the personal details to himself.

Styles and singer Taylor Swift take a walk through New York City in December 2012.

In August 2013, One Direction goes to a premier of their documentary *One Direction: This Is Us*.

When the band's second album, *Take Me Home*, came out in November 2012, they topped the *Billboard* chart for the second time that year. Throughout 2013, they toured and made their documentary, *One Direction: This Is Us*. The documentary gave fans a look behind the scenes. By then, Styles was more famous than he'd ever dreamed. But there was also a lot of pressure put on him. He had to sign contracts that had rules about his personal behavior, which made him nervous even though he had no plans to do anything wrong. He worried about making mistakes while performing. He even threw up before shows.

"At that point any natural confidence I had was being taken over by nerves because back then I had no idea how to channel and control my anxiety," he said.

In November, One Direction, also called 1D, released their third album, *Midnight Memories*. It was the UK's fastest-selling album of the year, with 237,000 copies sold in the first seven days. They hit the No. 1 spot on the *Billboard* chart once again.

By the time *Four* came out in 2014, the band topped the chart for the fourth time and their success was far from surprising. They worked well together, and despite the pressure, Styles felt grateful. He was especially happy to have such a strong bond with his bandmates.

"I feel really lucky that we always had each other to be this unit that felt like you could keep each other in check and you could just have someone else who gets it," he said.

After releasing their fourth album, *Four*, in 2014, One Direction played on NBC's *Today* show.

Together, Styles, Malik, Tomlinson, Horan, and Payne couldn't seem to fail. But in March 2015, it all came crashing down. Malik announced he was leaving. He was stressed and wanted to live a normal life with some privacy and time to relax. The rest of the band understood, but at the same time, they were surprised by this major decision. "We were sad that someone had left, but also sad that he was . . . not enjoying it so much that he had to leave," Styles said.

As the year continued, Styles, Horan, Tomlinson, and Payne kept touring. They bonded over losing Malik and planned to go on without him. But they needed to figure out how.

Styles signs autographs for fans in Japan in 2013.

In August, Styles and the other remaining band members decided to take a break. Directioners, as fans called themselves, worried, but Styles felt the break could be good for them too. "I didn't want to exhaust our fan base," he said. "If you're shortsighted, you can think, 'Let's just keep touring,' but we all thought too much of the group than to let that happen. You realize you're exhausted and you don't want to drain people's belief in you."

Stepping Out Solo

In November 2015, One Direction released their fifth album, *Made in the A.M.* Styles, Horan, Tomlinson, and Payne all had a hand in writing songs on the album. Even after the shake-up, they proved they were as dedicated as ever to their craft and their fans.

"I think it was obviously different, the process, because there was one less of us, but at the same time, it didn't change in terms of the writing of the album," Styles said. "I think the focus over the last five years has always been the same in that we want to make, you know, the best record we can."

Made in the A.M. was another hit. It turned out to be One Direction's last album as a band. In January 2016, Styles, Horan, Tomlinson, and Payne didn't renew their contracts with their record label. They decided to go their separate ways, and Styles looked forward to pursuing a career as solo singer and an actor.

Left to right: Styles, Horan, Payne, and Tomlinson released one more album, *Made in the A.M.,* as One Direction.

"I wanted to step up. There were songs I wanted to write and record," he said. "Every decision I've made since I was sixteen was made in a democracy. I felt like it was time to make a decision about the future . . . and maybe I shouldn't rely on others."

One of the first things he did was change his look by cutting off his famous long locks. He donated his hair to the Little Princess Trust, an organization that makes wigs for children who have hair loss as a result of cancer treatments. Soon after, in June 2016, he signed a recording contract with Columbia Records as a solo artist. When he found out he didn't have to sign anything related to his personal behavior, he was so relieved that he cried. "I felt free," he said.

Styles could finally take charge of his life and his career. He bought a new home in California and made plans to move in a direction that wasn't possible before. "I wanted to write *my* stories, things that happened to me," he said. "The number-one thing was I wanted to be honest."

He was excited to have a new band of musicians to work with. And he was nervous about putting out a solo album with a new sound. When his self-titled album, *Harry Styles*, was released in May 2017, *Variety* called him, "a sensitive soul . . . a serious pop performer with

Styles attends an iHeartRadio event in May 2017.

enviable vocal chops and a gifted ability to convey a song's emotional heft." The album topped the *Billboard* 200 albums chart and sold 193,000 albums in its first week in the UK. As a solo artist, Styles was a hit straight out of the gate.

Styles's album was an ambitious creative project. Three days after it came out, he also released his documentary *Harry Styles: Behind the Album* on Apple Music, so fans could see how he made it. He also found time to get involved in another opportunity. He sent an audition tape for the movie *Dunkirk*, then joined director Christopher Nolan to workshop the movie. Styles was cast as a British soldier in World War II (1939–1945) and loved getting to play a role.

After five years with One Direction, Styles was spreading his wings and showing the world he could fly solo. His career was off to a great start, and there was plenty more he wanted to do.

Getting Help

For a long time, Styles resisted the idea of therapy. But he struggled with anxiety, feeling closed off emotionally, and other mental health issues. In 2017 he decided to try therapy after all. It helped him work on things that he felt were holding him back.

On May 8, 2017, Styles performs at the iHeartRadio Album Release Party.

Owning His Voice and Style

Styles's solo career kept taking off. He purchased a penthouse in New York in early 2017. By September he'd left on a world tour, playing shows in North America, South America, Australia, Europe, and Asia. While on the stages, he expressed himself in more ways than one.

Not only did he put on a good show, Styles also supported LGBTQIA+ rights by selling T-shirts printed with the words "Treat people with kindness." He waved Black Lives Matter flags and put stickers on his guitar that read, "End gun violence." Throughout his tour, he raised $1.2 million to put toward charity donations. He supported water conservation efforts, registering people to vote, and charities focused on preventing sexual harassment.

"I'm not always super-outspoken. But I think it's very clear from choices that I make that I feel a certain way about lots of things," Styles said.

Styles's fashion evolved too. He went bolder than he had before and took to wearing brightly colored suits, satin flared pants, stacked heels, and lots of rings. His gender-fluid style allowed him to dress in clothes designed for all genders, and that attracted attention. But Styles was more interested in self-expression and inclusivity than labels.

"I think there's so much masculinity in being vulnerable and

Styles wore many fun outfits throughout his tour Harry Styles: Live on Tour in 2017 and 2018.

Styles performs at Madison Square Garden in New York City on June 21, 2018.

allowing yourself to be feminine, and I'm very comfortable with that," he said. "I definitely find—through music, writing, talking with friends, and being open—that some of the times when I feel most confident is when I'm allowing myself to be vulnerable."

Throughout 2018, his projects included music, modeling, and more. Working with singer-songwriters Jack Antonoff and Ilsey Juber, he cowrote "Alfie's Song (Not So Typical Love Song)" for the soundtrack of the movie *Love, Simon.* The same year, he produced a TV show called *Happy Together*, which was based on his life. It starred Damon Wayans Jr. and Amber Stevens West as a married couple, and Felix Mallard in the role of a young pop star.

He also modeled for Gucci in their men's tailoring campaign. To promote the brand, he dressed in a robe and carried a live chicken in one video and wore a headband and purple jacket while exploring sculptures in another.

Fans appreciated his openness, honesty, and his support. He even won the *Gay Times* LGBTQ Advocate Award for his efforts to make people feel accepted and seen at his shows. One way he did this was by waving Pride flags during his concerts. He wanted everyone at his shows to feel welcome, loved, and equal. As someone who felt very supported, Styles eagerly gave that same support right back.

Styles holds up a Pride flag during one of his concerts in 2018.

Styles takes the stage for the 2019 Capital's Jingle Bell Ball.

Styles Sets the Tone

By 2019 Styles had figured out how to hold back less and be himself even more. The shift helped his creative process. He wanted to share more of his feelings in his songs, including writing about his romantic relationships—particularly after a bad breakup. He didn't name names in his lyrics, but he put his pain into his songs.

Styles also got into meditation and found that helped him live in the moment and stay open emotionally, even when it wasn't easy. "I think meditation has helped with worrying about the future less, and the past less. I feel like I take a lot more in—things that used to pass by me because I was always rushing around," he said.

Two years after releasing his debut album, Styles was at work on his second album. In February 2019, he put out a video for a new song, "Falling." In it, he wore a chiffon Gucci dress while playing a piano erupting with water. The water eventually submerged him. For Styles, the video expressed ideas about being overwhelmed.

"You can feel like you're drowning sometimes in however you're feeling," he said. "It's like, writing these songs are what helps, but also they can hurt you sometimes."

Styles and designer Alessandro Michele at the 2019 Met Gala

While Styles leaned into pain in many of his new songs, he took a different approach to fashion. For him, it was all about fun. He proved his point that May when he showed up to cohost the Met Gala with tennis player Serena Williams, designer Alessandro Michele, and singer Lady Gaga. It was his first time attending the high-fashion fundraising event, and his look was over-the-top. He wore a sheer, black Gucci blouse with lace sleeves and a bow flowing down the front. He had a pearl earring dangling from one ear. His fingernails were painted black and teal, and he wore several rings on his fingers.

The same month, he released a video for another new song, "Watermelon Sugar." He'd written it while on tour in 2017, and this one was more upbeat. Filming took place on the beach on a hot day, and Styles had the job of having fun and flirting with a group of models. He aimed

Millions at the Met

The Met Gala was started in 1948 to raise money for a collection of clothing and accessories called The Costume Institute. Since 1971 it has been held each year at the Metropolitan Museum of Art in New York City. Each year the Met Gala has a theme. Stars that attend the event dress according to the theme. In 2022 the event raised over $17 million for the Institute.

Styles and tennis player Serena Williams (*center*) greet actress Awkwafina (*right*) at the 2019 Met Gala.

for a video that showed the excitement of being around someone new that you really like.

During the shoot, a director told him to play with model Ephrata's hair. But Styles didn't do it right away. First, he checked in with Ephrata and asked if it was OK with her. "That was a moment on-set where I was taken aback for just a second and was like, 'Wow, he really cares if I'm comfortable. He cares if the other models are comfortable,'" Ephrata said.

Styles was that kind of superstar—one who would ask for consent, respect boundaries, and set the right tone for everyone on his project. He could feel at ease while he did his best work, and those around him could too.

A Year of Self-Discovery

Styles released his second album, *Fine Line*, in December 2019. It instantly landed at the top of the *Billboard* 200 chart. By then, he had homes in California and London, but he was most comfortable touring and spent most of his time on the road. He was set to kick off his Love on Tour shows in April 2020.

But the worldwide COVID-19 pandemic stopped his plans. The US, England, and many other countries went into lockdown, closing businesses and schools and limiting travel. Styles was grounded at his home in Los Angeles. For the first time in years, his schedule was completely clear.

Style Icon

Styles is known for wearing brightly colored, flamboyant clothing. His look has been called fun, retro (imitating past fashions), and gender fluid. He says he's inspired by superstars including Gucci designer Alessandro Michele and music legends David Bowie, Elton John, Prince, and Shania Twain.

Styles wears a polka dot shirt during a concert in 2020.

In the beginning, he thought he should use the time to write more music. Soon, though, he saw it would be better to take a break. He and some friends socialized safely, so he had people to hang out with—and plenty of time to get to know them better. For about six weeks, he dug into that, getting closer to his friends and considering what it means to create deep friendships and a real home. After years of travel, Styles had a lot to think about.

When he started making music again, he used what he'd learned in lockdown. He wanted to make his third album even more personal. He didn't even listen to his favorite artists' music while he worked because he didn't want to be influenced by their songs. He only listened to classical music.

While 2020 was a hard year all over the world, Styles still managed to score some victories. He was cast in a new movie that was being directed by Olivia Wilde. He would star alongside Florence Pugh, Chris Pine, and Gemma Chan as well as Wilde. His single "Adore You" was the year's second-most-played song on the radio in the US. And his song "Watermelon Sugar" was No. 22 on *Variety*'s Hitmakers list.

Success in the US was good news, but Styles felt it

Left to right: Gemma Chan, Harry Styles, Sydney Chandler, Olivia Wilde, Chris Pine, Florence Pugh, and Nick Kroll attend a film premiere in 2020.

Styles sports a Gucci dress and jacket in a photo on the cover of *Vogue* in 2020.

was more important to stay committed to making the music he wanted to make. To him, that meant continuing to take creative risks and not worrying about popularity and writing hit songs.

In 2020, Styles and his sister, Gemma, modeled for *Vogue* together. When Styles appeared on the cover, he was the first man to do so solo. He took the moment to make a splash and a statement all at once. Wearing a Gucci jacket and dress, he was excited to break rules and reach beyond limits he had placed on himself before.

"What's really exciting is that all of these lines are just kind of crumbling away. When you take away 'There's clothes for men and there's clothes for women,' once you remove any barriers, obviously you open up the arena in which you can play," he said. "It's like anything—anytime you're putting barriers up in your own life, you're just limiting yourself."

Moving Forward with Freedom

In early 2021, after meeting on the set of actor and director Wilde's movie, Wilde and Styles started dating. Styles kept quiet about their relationship publicly.

They were still together in March when Styles went to the Grammy Awards with three nominations: *Fine Line* for Best Pop Vocal Album, "Adore You" for Best Music Video, and "Watermelon Sugar" for Best Pop Solo Performance. When he won his first-ever Grammy for "Watermelon Sugar," Wilde posted on Instagram to congratulate him. She put up a picture of singer Paul McCartney eating watermelon, along with a praising-hands emoji.

Styles's award was a milestone in more ways than one. He'd never won a Grammy before. And while he was at the ceremony, he realized something. Surrounded by new and younger performers, he remembered his own rise to fame. It was suddenly clear to him that trying to hang on to that experience would never be the right goal. Instead, he had to get comfortable finding other experiences that would make him happy. The realization gave him a new sense of freedom about his future.

"You can't win music," he said. "It's not like Formula One."

As the year continued, Styles didn't have to worry. He had plenty going on in his career, including acting in the Marvel movie *Eternals*. The following year, he launched Gucci HA HA HA, a clothing line he designed with his friend Alessandro Michele.

In May 2022, he released his third album, *Harry's House,*

At the 2021 BRIT Awards, Styles wins the Mastercard British Single Award for "Watermelon Sugar."

which featured his hit song "As It Was." Once again, he topped the *Billboard* 200 chart. He called it his most intimate album yet. And this time, he wasn't worried about what people thought of it.

"I just want to make stuff that is right, that is fun, in terms of the process, that I can be proud of for a long time, that my friends can be proud of, that my family can be proud of, that my kids will be proud of one day," he said.

Later that year Styles and Wilde went their separate ways. But in August, his delayed Love on Tour shows finally kicked off at Madison Square Garden in New York City.

Styles holds his 2023 Album of the Year and Best Pop Vocal Album Grammy Awards.

Styles performs in 2021 during one of his Love on Tour shows.

Styles had even more exciting news ahead of the 2023 Grammy Awards. "As It Was" was had four nominations and *Harry's House* had two. On February 5, he won Album of the Year and Best Pop Vocal Album.

Over years in the spotlight, Styles learned how to harness his talents and create beautiful music. He got comfortable speaking his truth and tapping into his emotions. And he stood up for his beliefs while guarding his own privacy. He has all the pieces in place to continue singing, acting, and creating the inclusive world he envisions.

IMPORTANT DATES

1994   Harry Styles is born on February 1.

2010   He auditions for the UK version of *The X Factor*.

2011   He releases his first album with One Direction.

2015   Zayn Malik leaves One Direction.

2017   Styles releases his debut solo album and appears in the movie *Dunkirk*.

2018   Styles wins the *Gay Times* LGBTQ Advocate Award.

2019   Styles releases his second album, *Fine Line*.

2020   The COVID-19 global pandemic spreads.

Styles is the first man to appear solo on the cover of *Vogue*.

2021   Styles wins a Grammy award for "Watermelon Sugar."

2022   He releases his third album, *Harry's House*.

He launches his Gucci HA HA HA clothing line.

He kicks off his tour Love on Tour.

SOURCE NOTES

9 "Harry Styles Wins Best Pop Solo Performance," YouTube video, 2:16, posted by Recording Academy/GRAMMYs, March 14, 2021, https://www.youtube.com/watch?v=UlIq5gvqOmA.

9 Hamish Bowles, "Playtime with Harry Styles," *Vogue*, November 13, 2020, https://www.vogue.com/article/harry-styles-cover-december-2020.

12 Tina Benitez-Eves, "16-Year-Old Harry Styles' Previously Unseen 'X-Factor' Audition Unearthed," *American Songwriter*, accessed November 14, 2022, https://americansongwriter.com/16-year-old-harry-styles-previously-unseen-x-factor-audition-unearthed/.

13 "Harry Styles Audition: EXTENDED CUT," YouTube video, 6:07, posted by The X Factor UK, accessed July 30, 2022, https://www.youtube.com/watch?v=p_VssaTwwLY&tt=1s.

15 Sara Netzley, "New *X Factor* Footage Shows How One Direction Were *Really* Formed—with Liam Payne Expected to be 'the Leader,'" *Entertainment Weekly*, July 23, 2022, https://ew.com/music/one-direction-formation-x-factor-unseen-footage-released-liam-payne/.

15 "One Direction—Judges House," YouTube video, 6:05, posted by TheOnly1Direction, March 11, 2012, https://www.youtube.com/watch?v=lHrzBKfwrlU.

20 Ariel Nagi, "Even Harry Styles Has Struggled with Self-Confidence: "I Had No Idea How to Control My Anxiety,'" *Seventeen*, September 23, 2014, https://www.seventeen.com/celebrity/a28387/harry-styles-confidence-issues-anxiety/.

21 "Harry Styles Discusses 'Deep Love' One Direction Bandmates Share 6 Years After Hiatus," Capital FM, May 17, 2022, https://www.capitalfm.com/news/harry-styles-one-direction-bandmates/.

22 "Harry Styles Gets Candid about Zayn Malik Leaving One Direction," YouTube video, 3:14, posted by *Entertainment Tonight*, November 22, 2019, https://www.youtube.com/watch?v=hX6ytGBe81Y.

23 Luke Morgan Britton, "Harry Styles Explains Why He Wanted One Direction to Take a Break and Speaks About Possible Reunion," *NME*, April 18, 2017, https://www.nme.com/news/music/harry-styles-one-direction-hiatus-reunion-2054324.

23 "Part II: The Adventures of One Direction & @COUPDEMAIN!" YouTube video, 14:30, posted by coupdemainmagazine, October 17, 2015, https://www.youtube.com/watch?v=URw-mAixppA.

24   Cameron Crowe, "Harry Styles' New Direction," *Rolling Stone*, April 18, 2017, https://web.archive.org/web/20180713193059/https://www.rollingstone.com/music/music-features/harry-styles-new-direction-119432/.

25   Lou Stoppard, "Exclusive: Harry Styles Reveals the Meaning Behind His New Album, 'Harry's House'," *Better Homes & Gardens*, April 26, 2022, https://www.bhg.com/better-homes-and-garden-magazine/harry-styles/.

25   Crowe.

25–26   Eve Barlow, "Harry Styles' Solo Album: A Track-By-Track Breakdown," *Variety*, May 12, 2017, https://variety.com/2017/music/news/harry-styles-solo-album-track-breakdown-1202424544/.

28   Trey Taylor, "Harry Styles: The Boy Is Back," *The Face*, September 5, 2019. https://theface.com/music/harry-styles-feature-interview-music-stevie-nicks-elton-john-alessandro-michele-volume-4-issue-001.

28–29   i-D Magazine, "Timothée Chalamet Meets Harry Styles," *Vice*, November 2, 2018, https://www.vice.com/en/article/evwwma/timothee-chalamet-in-conversation-with-harry-styles-the-hottest-actor-on-the-planet-interviewed-by-musics-most-charismatic-popstar.

31   Rob Sheffield, "The Eternal Sunshine of Harry Styles," *Rolling Stone*, August 26, 2019, https://www.rollingstone.com/music/music-features/harry-styles-cover-interview-album-871568/.

32   "Harry Styles Takes Us Behind the Drenched Video for 'Falling,'" YouTube video, 1:06, posted by Audacy Music, March 1, 2020, https://www.youtube.com/watch?v=mCVe3Yvl6K8.

34   Dana Gerber, "The 'Watermelon Sugar' Music Video Models Just Told Us Everything About Working with Harry Styles," *Cosmopolitan*, July 8, 2020, https://www.cosmopolitan.com/entertainment/music/a32982410/harry-styles-watermelon-sugar-music-video-behind-the-scenes/.

37   Bowles.

38   Stoppard.

40   Stoppard.

SELECTED BIBLIOGRAPHY

Barlow, Eve. "Harry Styles' Solo Album: A Track-By-Track Breakdown." *Variety*, May 12, 2017. https://variety.com/2017/music/news/harry-styles-solo -album-track-breakdown-1202424544/.

Benitez-Eves, Tina. "16-Year-Old Harry Styles' Previously Unseen 'X-Factor' Audition Unearthed." *American Songwriter*, accessed October 24, 2022. https://americansongwriter.com/16-year-old-harry-styles-previously -unseen-x-factor-audition-unearthed/.

Bowles, Hamish. "Playtime with Harry Styles." *Vogue*, November 13, 2020. https://www.vogue.com/article/harry-styles-cover-december-2020.

Crowe, Cameron. "Harry Styles' New Direction." *Rolling Stone*, April 18, 2017. https://www.rollingstone.com/feature/harry-styles-new-direction-119432/.

Gerber, Dana. "The 'Watermelon Sugar' Music Video Models Just Told Us Everything About Working with Harry Styles." *Cosmopolitan*, July 8, 2020. https://www.cosmopolitan.com/entertainment/music/a32982410/harry -styles-watermelon-sugar-music-video-behind-the-scenes/.

Nagi, Ariel. "Even Harry Styles Has Struggled with Self-Confidence: 'I Had No Idea How to Control My Anxiety.'" *Seventeen*, September 23, 2014. https:// www.seventeen.com/celebrity/a28387/harry-styles-confidence-issues -anxiety/.

Recording Academy/GRAMMYs. "Harry Styles Wins Best Pop Solo Performance, 2021 GRAMMY Awards Show Acceptance Speech." YouTube, March 14, 2021. https://www.youtube.com/watch?v=UlIq5gvqOmA.

Sheffield, Rob. "The Eternal Sunshine of Harry Styles." *Rolling Stone*, August 26, 2019. https://www.rollingstone.com/music/music-features/harry-styles -cover-interview-album-871568/.

Stoppard, Lou. "Exclusive: Harry Styles Reveals the Meaning Behind His New Album, 'Harry's House.'" *Better Homes & Gardens*, April 26, 2022. https:// www.bhg.com/better-homes-and-garden-magazine/harry-styles/.

Taylor, Trey. "Harry Styles: The Boy Is Back." *The Face*, September 5, 2019. https://theface.com/music/harry-styles-feature-interview-music-stevie-nicks -elton-john-alessandro-michele-volume-4-issue-001.

LEARN MORE

Bach, Greg. *Harry Styles*. Hollywood, FL: Mason Crest, 2023.

Biography: Harry Styles
    https://www.biography.com/musician/harry-styles

Hameenaho-Fox, Satu. *Be More Harry: Authentic Advice on Subverting Expectations and Embracing Kindness*. New York: Dorling Kindersley Limited, 2022.

Harry Styles Official Website
    https://www.hstyles.co.uk

Huddleston, Emma. *Harry Styles*. Lake Elmo: Focus Readers, 2021.

One Direction Official Website
    https://www.onedirectionmusic.com/gb/home.html

Recording Academy Grammy Awards: Harry Styles
    https://www.grammy.com/artists/harry-styles/287522

Schwartz, Heather E. *Taylor Swift: Superstar Singer and Songwriter*. Minneapolis: Lerner Publications, 2019.

INDEX

PHOTO ACKNOWLEDGMENTS

Images used: TIZIANA FABI/AFP/Getty Images, p. 4; Kevin Winter/The Recording Academy/Getty Images, p. 6; Amy Sussman/The Recording Academy/Getty Images, p. 8; Mark Waugh/Alamy Stock Photo, p. 10; ARCHIVIO GBB/Alamy Stock Photo, p. 11; David M. Benett/Getty Images, p. 12; Ian Gavan/Getty Images, pp. 13, 16; Dominic Lipinski/PA Images/Getty Images, p. 14; Toni L. Sandys/The Washington Post/Getty Images, p. 18; David Krieger/Bauer-Griffin/Getty Images, p. 19; Lars Niki/Corbis/Getty Images, p. 20; Olivia Salazar/FilmMagic/Getty Images, p. 21; Visual China Group/Getty Images, p. 22; Victor Chavez/WireImage/Getty Images, p. 24; Dimitrios Kambouris/Getty Images, pp. 25, 27; Steve Jennings/Getty Images, p. 28; Kevin Mazur/Getty Images, pp. 29, 30, and 35; Isabel Infantes/PA Images/Getty Images, p. 31; James Devaney/ GC Images/Getty Images, p. 32; Matt Winkelmeyer/MG19/Getty Images, p. 33; Vittorio Zunino Celotto/Getty Images, p. 36; AP Photo/Charles Guerin/Abaca/Sipa USA, p. 37; JMEnternational/JMEnternational for BRIT Awards/Getty Images, p. 39; Alberto E. Rodriguez/Getty Images, p. 40; Anthony Pham/Getty Images, p. 41.

Cover: Dave J Hogan/Getty Images.